MY FIRST

MOROCCO

ALL ABOUT MOROCCO FOR KIDS

GL●BED
CHILDREN BOOKS

Interior and cover Design: Daniel Day
Editor: Margaret Bam

For My Sons, Daniel, David and Jude

Marrakesh, Morocco

Morocco

Morocco is a **country**.

A country is land that is controlled by a **single government**. Countries are also called **nations, states, or nation-states**.

Countries can be **different sizes**. Some countries are big and others are small.

Camels in the Sahara desert

Where Is Morocco?

Morocco is located in the continent of **Africa.**

A continent is **a massive area of land that is separated from others by water or other natural features**.

Morocco is situated in the northern part of Africa.

Hassan Tower, Rabat, Morocco

Capital

The capital of Morocco is Rabat.

Rabat is located in the **northern part** of the country.

Casablanca is the largest city in Morocco.

Medina, Marrakesh, Morocco

Regions

Morocco is divided into 12 regions

The regions of Morocco are as follows

Tanger-Tétouan-Al Hoceïma, Oriental, Fès-Meknès Rabat-Salé-Kénitra, Béni Mellal-Khénifra, Casablanca-Settat, Marrakech-Safi, Drâa-Tafilalet, Souss-Massa, Guelmim-Oued Noun, Laâyoune-Sakia El Hamra and Dakhla-Oued Eddahab.

Moroccan woman making bread

Population

Morocco has a population of **37.9 million people** making it the 11th most populated country in Africa and the 39th most populated country in the world.

Casablanca is Morocco's most populated city, with a population of around 3.7 million people. Around 35% of Morocco's population lives in rural areas.

Chefchaouen, Morocco

Size

Morocco is **710,850 square kilometres** making it the 39th largest country in the world by area and the 18th largest country in Africa.

Morocco has a diverse landscape that includes rugged mountains, coastal plains, and desert regions. The Atlas Mountains, which run through the centre of the country, are a popular tourist destination.

Languages

The official languages of Morocco are **Arabic and Amazigh.** The Arabic language is spoken by hundreds of million people around the world.

There are regional languages spoken in Morocco; these are Moroccan Arabic, Hassaniya Arabic, Berber and French.

Here are a few Moroccan phrases and sayings

- **As-salaam Alaykum** - Hello
- **Labas?** - How are you?

Hassan II Mosque, Morocco

Attractions

There are lots of interesting places to see in Morocco.

Some beautiful places to visit in Morocco are

- **Hassan II Mosque**
- **Koutoubia**
- **Jardin Majorelle-Yves Saint Laurent Mansion**
- **Jamaa el Fna Square**
- **Bahia Palace**
- **Ouzoud Falls**

The magnificent fort of the Kasbah Ait Benhaddou

History of Morocco

Morocco has a rich and complex history, with influences from various cultures and civilizations over time. The region has been inhabited since prehistoric times, and has been ruled by Berber dynasties, Arab dynasties, and European powers over the centuries.

Idris I of Morocco established the first Moroccan state in 788.

Morocco gained independence on 7th April 1956.

Fes, Morocco

Customs in Morocco

Morocco has many fascinating customs and traditions.

- Moroccans are known for their warm hospitality and welcoming nature.
- Ramadan is an important religious event in Morocco. During this time, Muslims fast from sunrise to sunset and break their fast with a meal called iftar.
- Henna is a natural dye that is used to create intricate designs on the skin. It is often used for weddings and other special occasions.

Moroccan musician

Music of Morocco

Music is an important part of Moroccan culture, with a variety of traditional and contemporary styles. Popular music genres in Morocco include Gnawa music, Arabic music, Berber music, Andalusi classical music, Chaabi, Raï and Malhun.

Some notable Moroccan musicians include
- Mahmoud Guinia
- Hassan Hakmoun
- Ammouri Mbarek
- Mehdi Nassouli

Moroccan Couscous

Food of Morocco

Moroccan food is known for being tasty, delicious and flavoursome.

The national dish of Morocco is **cous cous,** a delicious dish made with small steamed granules of rolled semolina.

Tagine

Food of Morocco

Moroccan cuisine is known for its spices, such as cumin, cinnamon, and saffron, as well as its use of fruits and vegetables, such as apricots, dates, and eggplant.

Some popular dishes in Morocco include

- **Tagine - A slow-cooked stew made with meat, vegetables, and spices**
- **B'stilla - A savoury pastry filled with chicken and almonds**
- **Kefta - Spicy meatballs made with ground beef or lamb, herbs, and spices**

Tanneries, Marrakesh, Morocco

Weather in Morocco

Morocco has a **Mediterranean climate**, with mild winters and hot summers. The coastal areas tend to be cooler and wetter, while the interior and desert regions are hot and dry.

Morocco experiences seasonal winds known as the "trade winds," which can affect weather patterns.

The wettest months in Morocco fall between November to March.

Animals of Morocco

There are many wonderful animals in Morocco.

Here are some animals that live in Morocco

- **Cuvier's gazelle**
- **Barbary macaque**
- **Northern bald ibis**
- **Egyptian vulture**
- **Berber toad**

Sports in Morocco

Sports play an integral part in Moroccan culture. The most popular sport is **Football.**

Here are some of famous sportspeople from Morocco

- **Achraf Hakimi - Football**
- **Romain Saïss - Football**
- **Adel Taarabt - Football**
- **Mehdi Carcela - Football**
- **Hakim Ziyech - Football**
- **Sofiane Boufal - Football**

King Mohammed VI

Famous

Morocco has produced many notable people in various fields.

Here are some notable Moroccan figures

- **Mohammed Achaari – Writer**
- **King Mohammed VI - Monarch**
- **Gad Elmaleh – Comedian**
- **Armand Amar – Composer**
- **French Montana – Music Artist**
- **Michel Qissi – Actor**

Golden door of Royal Palace in Fes, Morocco

Something Extra...

As a little something extra, we are going to share some lesser known facts about Morocco

- Morocco is home to the world's oldest university, the University of Karueein.
- The Moroccan city of Casablanca is home to the largest artificial port in the world.
- Morocco is the world's largest exporter of sardines.
- The Moroccan city of Marrakech has the largest traditional market (souk) in the world.
- Morocco is known for its beautiful and intricate architecture.

Words From the Author

We hope that you enjoyed learning about the wonderful country of Morocco.

Morocco is a country rich in culture and beauty, with lots of wonderful places to visit and people to meet.

We hope you continue to learn more about this wonderful nation. If you enjoyed this book, consider leaving a review!

With Love